Babel's Stair

Babel's Stair

Poems by Rhoda Janzen

Word Press

Published by Word Press
P.O. Box 541106
Cincinnati, OH 45254-1106

Typeset in Goudy Old Style by WordTech Communications LLC,
Cincinnati, OH

ISBN: 1933456523
LCCN: 2006940438

Poetry Editor: Kevin Walzer
Business Editor: Lori Jareo

Visit us on the web at www.word-press.com

Author photo: Shelley LeLonde, Face Photography, Grand Haven,
MI

Cover image: "The Haywain," Hieronymus Bosch, from the panel
"Hell." Used by permission of the Museo del Prado.

Acknowledgements

American Literary Review: "Tardy Elegy." *Antigonish Review*: "Psalter Fool," "Why I am Not an Insect." *Buffalo Carp*: "Deceitful Beyond All Cure" and "The Suicides." *Cairn*: "Michigan Grand Prix." *Christian Century*: "North Dakota Sestina," "Man Answers God," and "Seniors Witness Portent." *Cimarron Review*: "The Rebus." *Concrete Wolf*: "How We Unlove Our Heroes" and "The Pigs." *Connecticut River Review*: "Nocturne." *Copper Nickel*: "Frizzy Hair." *Crazyhorse*: "Early Train." *Firebush*: "Shadow's Pleasure." *Folio*: "Bikini Wax" and "Pants Man." *Front Range Review*: "Night Emissions." *Gettysburg Review*: "The Siege," "Bad Breath," "Winter Skin," "Pinched Nerve," "Plantar's Wart," and "Varicose Vein." *Good Foot*: "Variations on *der Schleif.*" *Ledge*: "Hospice." *Lichen*: "The Shiverin' Bits." *Malahat Review*: "The Bible Belt," "Point to the Pain with One Finger," "The Host," and "Hearts for the Taking." *Mennonite Life*: "Heavy Yellow Heads." *New Delta Review*: "Recurring Rash." *New Scriblerus*: "Green Man in Good Neighborhood" and "The Unselected." *Perspectives*: "The Aunts by Firelight." *Poetry Midwest*: "The Fair" and "Man and Venn." *Poet's Touchstone*: "Broken Talus," "Why I Am Right for the Job," and "What To Save." *Salt River Review*: "Lunch without Genius." *So To Speak*: "Frown Line." *Talking River Review*: "Blonde Beast on the Move." *Tower Poetry Review*: "Small Town with Hush." *Vallum*: "Intelligence Test." *Valparaiso Review*: "First Time." *Vermilion Literary Project*: "The Maiden Box." *Windhover*: "The Bargain," "Graffiti Analyst Declines Honorarium," and "Sunday Storm." *Yale Review*: "Inhabited D."

"The Witch of Endor Game" appeared in *New Voices: University and College Poetry Prizes 1989-1998*, ed. Heather McHugh (Academy of American Poets, 2002).

for Joanne Jenkins

when it's twilight on the prairie

Contents

Inhabited D

Leaf from a twelfth-century sacramentary. The inhabited initial, which contains an illustrative scene or figure, was derived from the Byzantine interest in narrative.
—The J. Paul Getty Museum

Like a decorous swimmer you test
the world outside your D. Is language
then so easy to bear? Your D shells

your narrow shoulders, poised for retreat
in case the sentence into which you
have maneuvered is tiresome or dangerous.

How do you design your view, with its illuminare
so deucedly gold? That tendril of filigree
tickling your hat? A sacramentary denizen,

devotee of diffidence, must commence some praise
of Christ, your neighbor in the word. Or is
your interior too fretted with script,

damask drapes, damson drawing room?
You men of letters remind me it's time
to pay my calls, to entertain, to correspond

devoutly with those whose residence you recall.
Careful, piccolino: the nobleman with heavy
plume and shadowed chin would love to invite

you out, himself in. Then where you would be—
homeless? Damnified, or keeping house
with Lord of Arguments, who seeks, I hear,

a D for personal definition? What is
your mission, if you must depart? At least
lock up. Your domestic D is half a world
of comfort and could attract difficulty.
Perhaps you venture out simply to return
to depth as some in recent centuries

shore pages in foam, the waves' declension
dreams, dreaming, dreamt, where no traveler
speaks our salt. Desiccate, unlettered land.

Why I'm Right for the Job

Folding underwear in symmetrical
squares of three, blackblackblack,
thongthongthong, strikes a heartnote
of ease. From early childhood I trained
in pews that I'd lemon oiled the day

before. I stiffened Sunday mornings,
with my washboard spine (hands folding
silence into sunshine while the sermon
looped like a cumbersome bee.) I
rearranged nothing, drew no squiggles

on no bulletin, did not accost the tiny
cups for grape juice. Face like a hush,
interior licked by flame, I remained, yet
was consumed, a burning bush. Consider
as well my fashion years. The braided

chutes of youth had come undone, huge,
accidentally spectacular: pure cold flume
that took me to the banquet of the world.
Still my greatest pleasure was holding
still for photographers. Rotate your chin

ten degrees to the left, do not move, do
not move, hold it, freeze it, hold that
mouth. Oh, prayer!—I can pray without
moving a muscle. I can stare any god
right out of the room. Budge me, and I

will loose a glacier that cuts inchmeal
through your centuries. Heaviness
is mine to command. I am the mother
of frozen monoliths, spook-white,
inexorable, and still in my Sunday clothes.

Why I Am Not an Insect

*I tell you solemnly, that I have many times tried to
become an insect...*
—Dostoyevsky, *Notes from the Underground*

At sleep's threshold, threadlike
antennae silver the skin, probing

knowledge like a stickiness. The light
lace of a wing fans an exposed

shoulder; the dull bulk emits
a sigh. The insect considers

this a triumph. Who knows how
many times its pale green torque

will skim off for another pleasurable
landing? Here a plump earlobe

invites a message heard in sleep:
one hand brushes the bare breast

strayed above blankets, strangely
cooled until it is otherworldly,

marmoreal, the temperature of shale
in the shade. The body casts and

retrieves its lunar thorax, heaving
dumb slumber, too huge to know

that its members have been stranded
in the night air. The breast slopes

under the insect's touch, heat long
gone, a forgotten figure made

of snow that lists gradually earth-
ward, mute in ignorance and ice.

Deceitful Beyond All Cure

Snug as a swim-cap, the cat on your head avers,
Idling would stall any engine but mine.
Risk is to fear what worship is to shrine,
replies the beaded naval ornament. The cat purrs,
etcetera, in the direction of the beads. *Form*
follows function! say the beads (green, idyllic).
The blanket interrupts the cat with warm acrylic:
Detachment, of course, protects the charm
of anagnorisis. The paw on your lobe's pure
as a square or a post-it note: funeral at eight,
wake at six, dead at forty-four. *Where's the wait:*
the heart, you say, *is deceitful beyond all cure.*
A trench coat parts the blinds like legs—goddamn,
it's only daylight getting hard for one more ma'am.

How We Unlove Our Heroes

Consider how we unlove our heroes.
We fall in love with Wagner. And then dense
as Nietzsche, we wait gloved in an immense
drawing room, concentrating on our prose.
Naturally faith flourishes like fiction.
One of Cosima's chickens rustles in,
dressed absurdly in a crinoline,
twittering to set the cracked addiction.
Clucks breezy as a hostess dropping hints.
You know how you try not to read ahead,
but how the last word is already read?
It's like the dawn, all vicious innocence—
and implicated by the very word
that crashes like a high-toned Wagner chord.

Pants Man

Round beards dipped four-part harmony
on the bustling corner of Wells and Halstead.
They sang robustly, the women cementing
their eyes to the sidewalk. But the men

seemed verily to dare the world's contempt
with their witness, pants too short, beards
too long, homemade, handmaid, their simplicity
an upright middle digit to city shoppers. *Nun*

danket alle Gott, they sang, savoring the scorn.
A man laden with art supplies declined a tract.
But the Mennonite waved the tract noseward,
a carton of milk gone bad, the peculiar pleasure

of soured sin. Then the artist's frustrated voice
rose above the song: *Just keep your religion
in your pants, man.* Not understanding,
the leader turned and gave the tract to me.

I took it for every word of every verse, for
the shirt I could baste eyes closed, for
the scalded jars of crab and quince that tell
the women their work is done and it is good.

I lied to this man's holy fringe, the cotton
whose seams my needle had doubled
for the field. My pants flared fire for sweat
and saddle, for the hymn that pumps its baritone

like rusty well-water, for the mind that stands
empty as a silo swept clean after harvest sales,
but smelling still to the little believer who holds
the broom of woodchips and of wheat.

The Maiden Box

The laughter of seven girls stirring pickles
in an open-air summer kitchen eddies
like the vaporous tang of brine, steam
softening their German. Tonight in identical
green moiré they will usher in the cake,

singing their parents' favorite hymn.
Harmony rises in damp tendrils,
a vinegar-sweet whiff from the pantry
of the familiar. They are young, it is warm,
their mother my cousin will be proud.

Matched like pearls, they will come rolling
into church, a box of maidens carrying
a cake. They hum and sweep, they sing
and stir, seven sisters whose harmony
trembles like the paper wings of a myth.

Wise yet simple, they slice cucumbers
that they themselves have picked. Raised
for man and temple, virginal but fucked,
they'll come singing in a white-hot flame
of blondeness, pale as a spider web. Each

will at her solo take a turn, standing tall
and rustling, green like corn. Then
the congregation standing, the cake
frosted and unbending, the song so sternly
ending, "*Lobet! Preiset den Herrn!*"

Sunday Storm

Like the small
plastic action figures
that sometimes

choke the vacuum,
she stood feet apart,
as if walking in

the deserted street.
Windows frowned,
dark as the hoods

of holy inquisitors.
By *she* I mean *I*.
And the wings of

my coat flapped
backward, a weird
and broken bird.

From the bank
a woman ran in slow
motion to her car,

shouting I don't
know what. Her
umbrella whipped

the sky, which
opened up, saying,
By *you* I mean *her*.

Hospice

A late breeze rustles the tarp;
the workers have gone home.
I am surprised every day
by how fast they work:
walls up, windows in,
a shrubbery flourishing.

Inside, the rooms repeat
like nascent cells that cluster
and divide. The familiar tang
of sawdust screws into my nose,
pale odor of a construction
that levels as it builds.

Mornings when I leave
I'm sufficiently robust
to excite attention. Or
maybe it's boredom that clamps
the construction crew to me,
though I can hardly reconcile that

these same guys, whooping over
the usual curves, assembled
the stairway that races its fragile
beat of steps like hearts—
time running out, completion
nearing, project almost done.

As a kid I loved construction,
the happy promise of corrugated
tin stacked sociably along

the dry wall, the hortatory
bolts. But I no longer pass
the site without blocks

of panic, the first to dread
the courtesy of change. Rentfree,
soon the rooms will welcome
forfeiture, loss, our modern plagues,
guests on one elbow in narrow cots,
staring out the window, wondering

whose cat and is it loved?
Into the body's delicate closet
they shrink, stacking against
the door their souvenirs of sadness,
their piles of mismatched vinyl suitcases.

Lunch Without Genius

If it is a world without genius,
It is most happily contrived.
—Wallace Stevens

We split the bill without
pretending. Like adults
too heartily abroad
in Disneyland, I'm up
for suckering myself:
I haven't passed the prime
of disillusionment.
But the next morning in
the loamy patch of pale

cucumber seedlings I
considered the bad lunch
with only featherweight
chagrin, the same bite-sized
sting you get from watching
fierce Wundertots on *Star
Search*—when some little spud,
hair plastered with Vital-
is, lets'er rip with, Won't

You Come Home Bill Bailey?
My friend the optimist
says, Don't think of yourself
as contrived; think of your-
self as self-constructed.
Ergo my construct of

the lunch is positive:
it features me for some
days afterward knocking

mud off my garden shoes
and humming, Come on home
Bill Bailey, like an old
curvaceous sexbomb, some
Carrousel Club chanteuse
with marcelled wigs and a
contralto song about
my baby, the soul of
romance, who done me wrong.

The Blonde Beast on the Move

The bustling depot of her mind salutes
the slaves of sin and death, whose wage palls
with blonde solicitude. Now Beast commutes.
The train, punctual as Wagner, calls
the platinum chignon to rage for space,
anticipating the final station,
where jumbo bobbi pins can queer the race.
Call it what you will, this ideation—
gas, lithium, pills, railway accident—
appalls the high-tech doors that slide the world
unsealed, a confidential document.
See, she's accessorized and fragrant, curled
and waxed, insured and partnered. Signs at x
for all the pleasures suicide rejects.

Seniors Witness Portent

I was driving with my friend the optimist
who despite her optimism had that afternoon
noticed at Ralph's that on her shopping list
she had scribbled *ground belief*. The moon,

star-like, airkissed the Hollywood jacaranda.
The unhappy geriatrics withheld applause,
sitting on what they wished was a veranda,
not the bald cement abutment that it was.

They were motionless after a matzo supper,
watching as on a stage a curse-hungry teen,
whose face was tossed like a crumpled wrapper
into our headlights and our panic of adrenaline:

he seized a bicycle and sheered it at our car.
It was one of L.A.'s casual cruelties, the faces
as from a hole punch, dispensable and sure,
the earth that roils with unnamed psychosis

just under the urban blanket we have tucked
around its bulk, the fault-finding and the path
seismic—oh, it's been coming, it's been sicked
on us, the six-toed nightblooming behemoth.

Intelligence Test

Put these events in the correct order.
A prostitute looks young next to his john;
his wee hotpants make him seem much shorter.
A chow crosses at the crosswalk and is gone.
Chrysanthemums and candles mark the spot
where last night the police chief's grand-daughter
was fatally (but accidentally) shot.
A wall announces Melia is hotter
than scorching hotties known from other fucks.
You order a tostada without beef
for a vagrant vegetarian in a tux.
A business guy is passing out a sheaf
of leaflets advertising his dot com.
For five bucks Mrs. Temple reads your palm.

Refulgent Sonnet

Wax paper creased beyond intended use;
the smell of *Grieben* wafting damp and pale,
a foot in your food, the noxious blast like news
from Mennonites whose pantries you inhale.
Shame fouls the mood, a whiff of savage fart,
cold cabbage smell unscrewed from a thermos
full of Borscht. *Accept the smell into your heart
like Jesus*, said my Borscht. *It will affirm us.*
Temptation's test, a hot lunch on a tray—
Cheese Strata and Wheat Roll with Butter Pat—
occasioned prayer for envy's cure, and pray
I did. O Hot Lunch! Lord, I wanted it!
Shame before envy, and pearls before swine:
the pottage course precedes the bread and wine.

The Unselected

The overhead bellylaughs its funhouse
pallor, a bath of lavender distortions
undulant as eels. Are *we* the smiling
fatsos tethered to the mirror, protesting
the chill with chickenflesh, hands'
friction spanking that lonely note

of warmth? In quasi-nudity we scrutinize
the unselected. We see in each
slashed price a heady harlequin,
the garment that might do the trick.
Last season's churls clash mutiny
against gallant upper arms. And women

hail hopeful reflections, as if curbside
telepathy to cabbies might get them home.
For each ensemble holds the door
to possibility: an escort, back stiff
as a nutcracker, draws out the chair, and
dialogue just touches the lips, a decorous

kiss of cheap champagne, a flute-like
laugh that murmurs modestly, *O! If I
could do it all again...* The dressing
room's wide open, a tarmac on the strip;
one shopper in fifties craft idles
gracious intimacy, her nylon panties

underslung, rectangular as a seat-back tray.
Under signature attar of roses, dugs roil
deflated as a pair of bean-shaped lungs.

She has the brio of confidence at bridge,
flourishing her trump with Chanel-like *haute*:
My Dear, it's perfect for an evening out!

Hand on hip, smile a hammock hanging limp,
she plays points that set the veins a-gossip
on her legs. Weird sooners, both—for do we
not assume discovery of sorrow among
the world's uncouth? And is there other
antidote than such rose perfume, racked

like clearance coats, fraying seams
at final mark-down? Do not the buttons
of the world chafe with unselected wounds?
Beyond these dressing rooms, twilight hems
our afternoons. Let us away to clip the threads,
by light of bargain moons.

The Siege

A woman asks if I can spare some coin.
I like the word *coin*. When I ask the woman
what she'll have, she wants tea with lemon.
a steady stream of shuffling hungry men

are encouraged by the woman's success.
I have to shake my head with guilty rigor;
who can afford to give to every beggar?
I don't even register the urgent loneliness

slipped into my pocket, the pink homemade card
that says, You Could Be My Lady Come True!
A Single Gent Wants To Go Out With You!
Lady, This Is No Joxe, I Give You My Word

Of Honor, This Is For Real! The card appears
when I am quiet on the train, en route
to Fresno. The Gent has drawn a Santa suit
beneath whose droopy hat a Santa leers.

Over the years I've known Craig to confide
that as a boy he slept hugging a feather pillow,
pretending it was a wife who would follow
his chimney-warm body, asleep at his side

with her thigh trapped deliciously under his—
no boy's dream of sex. He wanted long-term
wifeliness, the very wife who at the alarm
would snap back the covers with energetic ease,

make coffee, use all the hot water, feed the cat,
sort the laundry, and grade six papers before
he got up. When I just can't stand it anymore,
I tiptoe in to see how he can sleep so late;

in my absence he has tenderly, achingly hugged
the pillow to his chest. Suddenly my eyes sting
for the Single Gent, who must by now be letting
himself into his new bachelor flat, recently fogged

for chiggers and carpet fleas as part of the deal:
the pink paper as he left it, the roach motels,
the light on his answering machine in red drills
that anticipate the siege—no joke, this is for real.

Graffiti Analyst Declines Honorarium

Suddenly the fingers of a human hand appeared
and began writing on the plaster of the wall...
—Daniel 5:5

An anthropologist drives a shabby car to South
Central, where he befriends some gangbangers,
graffiti artists. One says, You wanna see

graffiti? Man, I'll show you graffiti. On the street
corner he whips off his shirt casually, as if
flicking the lid from a pen. Along his shoulders

Old Roman script bites deep letters into flesh:
SANTA MONICA, a saint revised, a town
displaced. Now in the city's broth of fog

spray paint and jerked syllables writhe out of sense.
Unlike the other documents, these are anonymous.
Yet one summons a stealthy image of young men

at night, swift, severe, tattooed, cleanly operating.
It has nothing to do with sex, though the girls
wait smoking in the car. Pure politics, it is

economy of expression, the broadcast that will bless
the edge of doom. The analyst can read it. He can
tell you what it means—MENE, TEKEL, PARSIN,

unsigned voice of wrath. Letters tight and furled
as new-hatched wings are lighting on the walls,
poised like flies to pulse and reconfigure. And there

will be an angry swarm, lettered and unlettered,
scripted and unscripted, signed and unsigned, saying,
Your days are numbered, readers. Your reign is

at an end. So concludes the analyst, who bows
to the scroll of applause and declines the honorarium
(though the audience is grateful and holds him in esteem).

The Witch of Endor Game

Now the green inkling of gas, thin
as irony. For heat, the oven offers
Bake or *Broil*, to which she turns
when evening shrieks along the street,
hearty Russians bustling a basketball,
a clutch in violent hilarious sneakers

who'll grow up to marry the rare man
for whose illness there's no cure. Then
there's the puzzle of the suit. One day
they'll mystify themselves by uncloseting
a preference for wearing their good suit
around the house, by secretly relishing

the formality that clings to navy
emphasis, until jeans and sweats sink
stone-like toward sediment, like verses
creased on the cusp of consciousness.
Ah, potent intentions! Erratic lights
leapfrog the hill, a swift three-leggèd

race before the pot-luck's whisked
to hampers and Evelyn Kasdorf blames
the Witch of Endor game on you
(and since the specter of the shaggy
head, Evelyn is believed by parents
who dispute the occult imagination).

This is the hour when concentration
swims with subtlety: when five murmurs
ambiguously to six, when the oven clicks

and contradicts, when across the hall
a man sometimes plays his answering
machine for company and it's only

a clinician's voice, impersonal as
an adult Christ. In the tidy kitchen
in the half-light, in the interstices
between reading and knowing what she's
read, the oven's warm threshold invites
her to conclude what she can eke

from discipline. Witches retire to
a temperate hell; the hour stretches
in her lap, mildly lifting its paw
to the future's softening pale, and
all along the block urgent girls
on phones are promising not to tell.

The Bargain

after Weldon Kees

Under the bed's cotton tunnel,
My nightgown's made of flannel,

Bunching damp around my middle.
My sister's much too little

To recognize the need for prayer.
From the darkness on the floor

The lamp's skinny shadow arm
Reaches for my lucky charm.

Now sweating agony, I drink the cup
To be beautiful when I'm grown up,

And seal the solemn bargain plea
Like Christ in dark Gethsemane.

At forty-four, I am a beauty blown,
often forgetting to change the channel
and watching with the volume turned way down.
When my neighbor limbers her soprano
(she boasts that she was twice Miss Illinois),
humiliation rills my eyes with tears.
I cannot explain it. I'm paranoid
since the attack, and now the steps one hears
in hallways seem indifferently evil,
the disembodied of our neighborhoods.

And who would not despair when the dry goods
cocoon, and one honey-colored weevil
becomes a legion, the corn meal moving?
Worms that caress, so little, so loving?

A paid bulimic once in itchy clothes,
I vomited before the fashion shows.

But I find memory in part obscured.
Hair falling out in tufts, nude as a bird

unnested, plaintively cold, bewitching
blue veins; airsick and violently pitching

between cities; smoked two reducing packs,
was photographed with breasts like flaccid sacks;

solicited, corseted, wind-fanned, taped;
much sought as wife or mistress as once hoped.

At forty-four I am a beauty blown.
I have no beauty. I desire none.

First Time

The sniff of wipers on the glass
insists, Get out, go on, get out.
The beautiful shock of a punch
assuages the reflexive flinch
and buttons up one's old raincoat
with fingers that tremble loose, or
thrill vaguely to the abuser.

The first bruise is like the first kiss,
right and proper to remember
forever, the white hot gasp
inhaled open-mouthed to the chest,
the taproot of shooting temper
that, like a gladiolus with the thrips,
rasps dry and secretive, and drops

sick in March. It's as serviceable
as the raincoat in whose pockets
sudden panic hunts for change
in headlights that cough yellow-orange
among Kleenex and movie tickets,
counting and recounting the cost,
impatient for a tardy bus,

which when it comes is packed with thrips,
crumb-white and weighing down the stem.
One defies them to crawl in closer,
shoving to the thorn on Wilshire.
(One nostril clears: smell of onion jam.)
Rain drags us. Our number swells,
inching home through Beverly Hills.

At home the freezer hints that somewhere
in the hoarfrost the thing is hidden.
There's no smart without blood's fool,
nor does pain even fissure the skull
until one remembers all of a sudden,
the trick that the swelling resists—
black-eyed peas, tiny frozen fists.

The Pigs

Here are your hip boots, here
is your whip, here a superb boldness
at facing facts. Now comes the rage

like hairline cracks. Angers sniff
the ground in fearsome packs,
casually defecating. The legion

will burst big skins, barking
at a moon that was. Bent above
the droppings, you'll wonder why

they smell of your own mouth. That
odor—is it heavy, is it sweet, will
it hatch? Wipe your breath on 911.

Here are the police, the police have
come. But the moon's gone in,
the blinds are down. Where are

the barkers now, my friend?
Loping on the shadow line.
Head over cliff, then roiling foam.

Box Sister of the Future

Privacy squatted in its underpants
inside a cardboard refrigerator box
that needed nothing. *The Best Loved
Illustrated Bible Stories* opened

magically to the same page every time.
In the distance Lot skittered like an ant
to the tiny hill of his salvation. Looking
over her shoulder was his ivory wife,

one pale hand stuck like a moth in her
still-dark hair, the other gathering
the folds of a shimmering tunic.
She stared in sudden shock, as if

apprehended in some crime. Then she
must have felt herself turning, a sandy
tingling, the silent suck in the vacuum
of an hourglass. Her lustrous pleading

eyes gazed right at mine, saying, Box
Sister of the Future, quick! Put your hand
to your brow in a posture of sublime
terror, while you still have the time.

Hearts for the Taking

The hours were bearded, and in the beard dander.
A sound came rolling, rolling like pearls
in the wood-paneled closet between sleep and waking
        from under our bed

like a frantic deck shuffled by that blackjack dealer
who nightly turns cards with bored sleight-of-hand:
it's hearts for the taking when you were expecting a
        hand somehow less red.

Sweet luck of the gods had come down to the cat
who batted the nestling, thumb-white and fine-boned,
the tiny wings rilling, the little beak buzzing,
        a toy run amok.

Came a quiet albeit tender disturbance,
neither sleeping nor dreaming but balling our pillows;
the must-laden lakehouse still smelled of reluctance.
        How still was the clock!

Rigid we lay there, waiting for sunrise over the water,
the masts pointing like fingers straight to the sky,
accusing and pointing, a red regret paddling
        its boat made of tin—

but an egret is coming, coming like Jesus, turning his neck
to groom for our sins. They jump from his back,
hold their breath and go swimming, buoyant as tourists
        in rubberized skin.

The Shiverin' Bits

Twilight and evening bell
—Alfred, Lord Tennyson

See what happens when you try
not to remember an advertising ditty,
try not to read the billboards placed by
some thoughtful editor in your pretty

margins. You're finally here on Lake Mac
kicking your feet to a distant boat's bell,
watching a pair of focused egrets attack
whatever lies under the water—or, hell,

maybe they're just grooming. The point is,
it's your shoreline, your beach, your neighbor
with the little-boy fountain taking a whiz,
the great reward of all your labor.

The chilled summer sky with its sweater
of clouds was just what you wanted:
the shiverin' bits as you opened your letter
from L.A.; a woody house a little haunted

by a crusty gent in creased serge pants;
to wake up wondering why those tiny lights spin;
to see the water ruffled up with romance
unrelenting as a spicy Harlequin.

It's like a dance with too much liquor:
the billboards roughly tap your shoulder,
so aggressive cutting in that you feel sicker,
such intoxicating vim that you feel older.

And it's not that you're a slow or dreamy dancer.
In the weird half-light the brashest billboards seem
altogether unaware of your saucy little cancer—
Jesus Lord of All, and Try Our Meat Supreme.

Small Town with Hush

Gone, L.A.'s soothing loop of car alarms,
domestic disputes, feet pounding
a flimsy ding-bat balcony—the red wail
of sirens trails exhaust, picks up distance

like a chopper's spotlight that fingers
the dark. Memory sniffs the evening.
It's come to retrieve some lately
thought of valuable, like a courteous

and noiseless squirrel. Every night at ten
a mournful train claims the same sorrow:
one complaint, one history. The night fan
wets the ear against the awful quiet. All

this brilliant Michigan green must be
growing out of us, throat fuzzing fungus,
invisible seeds lodging, spoor tornadoes
rumbling rain. Church lawns cast green

glances at each other—who's greener?
And everywhere the index fingers
of steeples shush the open mouth.
Once a pair of CRCs ambushed me

while I was outside trimming yarrow,
a father and a son who asked me if I knew
the Lord. Around us the first drops of
silence fell, and then it came down hard.

Night Emissions

It's like putting on a clammy swimsuit
when the body is already dry,
the same body whose youth dampens
knowledge of its own perfection.
The body says, fuck it, let's just
keep driving till we're out of gas—
Boca Grande with a gay friend,
having brought nothing except
a James novel. Musty rental, kirs
all afternoon, catfish on some dock.
Eyes blue as a plastic ice tray put back
in the freezer empty. We cocked

arms sunward, deploying James
to shield the glare. The afternoon
condensed its already laconic self
like a haiku dead-center on the page.
The friend jumped up: he couldn't
take the hot bright everlasting James
sentence that went on like a marriage
about which one knows too much.
He melted the sea. Cicadas swelled
and splashed the silence. Nothing
moved or happened. You've no way
of knowing that this moment, which

seems small as a mint, will stay
painfully fresh, will freshen
the next twenty years, will bead
the mouth of every nightmare.
It will extrude salt from tear, beat

from heart's yammer as it bevels
its toy clarity. Night emissions rub
the groove: cat couldn't scratch it,
boned like a lighthouse on the point,
blinking its stiletto red warning
to Penelope—push off, honey,
he's never coming home.

Green Man in Good Neighborhood

I

At 3:30 a.m. the guest bathroom fidgets
fever, ghostly and unfamiliar. Veins
marble the skin, nonfat-blue on white,
otherworldly as a formica countertop.
It is the parents' house. The climate
offers one damp hand, a stranger. Windows
yawn all night; July is a late show through
which one seeks to sleep. Outside a soapsud
moon cleans all the world above Al Pauls'
garage. Homes along this block square
shoulders at lawns so stiffly green.

II

The ferns look like topiary cough drops,
snug Sucrets, low as a cough suppressed
in church—the same church just around
the corner with its faint quiet threat
of Sundays. That afternoon, still feeling fine,
one might recline on the dense shaved lawn
and seduce Al Pauls' cat to rub one's thigh.
The shadow of the kumquat tempts
illustration, an ancient edifice whose
bas-relief's been blunted over time.

III

The linoleum's hardly to your taste
and the wallpaper gallops minatory florals:

it shouts, it husks, it swings you round.
It whirls some dervish dance when in fact
one cannot stand. Because the bathroom's
adjacent to the parents' room, eventually
the mother's hand taps the door
like a root, pushing through cranapple
and Imodium. She apologizes
for the rich cream sauce at supper.

How regrettable to have admitted a lack
of emotion altogether! *What about fear,*
she asks. *What about Satan?* Once
blackened hoary callouses goatfooted it
down the hall; razors puzzled cold
configurations. Recall the dreamstop
of the deep red eye. You sadly shake
your head, though you aren't sad. You
have no fear of Satan, nor thrill of God, nor
love of man. Even now the twisting of your
trunk as you lean unsound into your sickness

IV

shoots a fuzz of seedlings. Pale ribs petrify
a casement with carved medieval cornice:
the Green Man, from whose lips emerge
vines that creep and bloom above his head,
looping into frenetic Latin. Throbbing cutworms,
tendrils inch out of Green Man's ears,
and his eyes cry leaves and buds of leaves.

Lean your forehead on the window, which
although not cool is cooler than your skin.

From the parents' screen a conversation
is spreading, a low voice rich as loam
and a softer, white-magnolia voice against it.
Pinch your forehead and feel for pain.
If in the refulgent furrow between your brows
you detect a swell, a nub rising, a sprig
of fragrant lavender, they had best let you go

to the lawn and the cat and Al Pauls' moon,
where with care from the gardening crew
your limbs will extend a pergola, on which
you will sustain seasons and echoes of seasons
with the riots that sweep into spring,
the purple shouting masses of hysteria.

Some Last Word

The cat, supine at the computer,
luxuriously stretched his paw
onto the exclamation mark.
And the screen repeated its

frenzy line upon line, scrolling
like a rapid finger through
Leviticus, cursor stuttering
frissons of emotion, outrage,

shock, pleasure, *come se*.
Returning with my coffee, I
thought *!!!*, a dialogue of sorts.
At last the cat had spoken. At last

spring addresses the scholar into
whose ear is whispered the thumb-
thick blinking radical, pulled
from the earth with such force

you plump back on your etymology,
there it is, what you've been tugging,
long tuber of truth, corollaries like
tangles on Medusa, the whole clump

crumbed and rolled with earth.
It's pale, it's huge, it's a plantar
triumph. Strange white root
long as the heat-seeking foot

that in the night abuts your shin
when you're out cold. Wake up,
wake up, it has something to say.

Early Train

Behind a fog like a curtain
whisked around a hospital bed,
a train sobers a driver at the gate.
The windshield's fogging up,
the delicate breath of an invalid
thought to be dead—he cracks

the window; the train sighs
its wet humidity, a tearful
farewell. Night swirls down
an antiseptic drain. Suddenly
he becomes aware of headlights
waiting on the other side, lights

that seem somehow personal,
white light that fidgets dread
of rendezvous. The barricade
arm snaps up like an Oldenburg
marker on some extravagant set,
scene over, extras gone home,

the director recognizing
a fancy sadness that fails to
shoot the thing again. If the sky
briefly clears its throat of fog,
he'll see a petri dish moon,
quietly containing its virus

with a little pox of stars,
keeping itself to itself,
yawning, perhaps, in light

languor, as if morning were
a further contamination and
dawn the season's cliffhanger.

The Suicides

Two young men
I almost loved
and a girl I knew

only in envy
(her hair tinted,
her dates lettered,

her person
lemon-scented)
have gone but now

they're back. They
wake the smallest
hours, a hand

pleating the sheet,
a chronic excited
whispering, a dying

to tell. Dying
told of having lived,
my pale ones,

my lining, Joe
and George and
Laurie, crowding

the moonlight,
those faces shining
lustrous and private,

like children
inventing their own
bedtime story.

Bikini Wax

White flags surrender gently to the low
sweet suck of gravitas: can't get a Rio
in western Michigan, *tableaux meurent*
of rag dolls, bushful marys, crotchable
full panties. Sara smears hot wax

like frosting on a cupcake; sprinkles talc
as on a wholesome changing table; snows
an innocence on rubble, follicles
revealed. (In one township there's a group
that opposes tampons, Satan's cotton fingers,

seeks solace in the wingèd panty shield.)
Note: Ladies Are Requested To Please Keep
Their Panties On.
                    The wax zig-jags a patch
of fjords, topography of risk. You give
up some things, some things give you up. A friend

develops violent intolerance
for wheat. Cards: inguinal hernia, cysts,
disks, kidney stones. A cousin's holiday
newsletter: a smidge too much about his prostate.
We wax for privacy. O modest Mich-

igonians, family-motored Christians,
the way of wax softens the heart, cries salt
for our incisions: pink and hairless,
a tenderness suturing bald forfeiture,
the thorn that frets the tweezed and wizened rose.

The Fair

From the front seat comes
my sister's voice like water
plashing stones. The pale roots

of her voice have taken hold
and are spreading. Miles fall away,
bold pennies dropped from the

Eiffel Tower, rushing oblivion,
unrecoverable. Once it was my task
to brush this sister's fog-white hair

before bed. I smoothed out fisted
rubber bands, the kink easing
the page-straight transparency

between us. At the airport, dawn
wheels the night away, a sturdy
miniature suitcase. My sister

pours juice into red plastic cups
sited on the fender like duck targets
at the Fresno Fair: all the new milk

you could gulp for a dime, a piano-
playing chicken's two-four thrill.
A sideshow barker shouted after

our whipsmart wheatlong braids,
Last chance, Blondie! If you
don't see it now, you never will.

Man and Venn

A man dropped out
of grad school when
the topic of a three-hour
seminar turned out to be,
Do Cats Plan? It seems

the man was indifferent
to cats and their putative
lists, their naïve optimisms,
their moments of ennui.
This man has since

failed at living. One might
not recognize his former
blade-thin brilliance in
his parabola of despair.
Given: the world opens

like an obsolescent
math book that refers
the reader to Figure 21-12,
where three or four
sky-blue puzzle pieces

snug the shaded area
of a Venn diagram—
the answers are
in the back of the book,
go on, just turn to the end.

Michigan Grand Prix

The sky bites its lips for a Judas
kiss: riders revving up like soldiers
in a reckoning rain. Noise flaps,

a checkerboard awning. Engines
throat the hill. On the curve they
swoop the asphalt, each pushing

the other down, sliders sparking,
dominoes that trip their own gestalt.
Track's center shrieks its homemade

kazoo, buzzing the lips with plastic
stretched across a man's wide
hum. Fast perfects loud. Now

down the straightaway stunt riders
thrill the ambulance with politics
of race that tense the fall. A girl

in low-rise pants waves her violent
titties at the crowd—Jesus in
a haltertop, she'll smoke them all.

The Bible Belt

The black belt coiled a drawer of ironed
white hankies that I myself had starched
and folded in sixths. Under a green
whiff of Binaca, vast dadpants lay,
so thin across the seat that you could
see right through to the sun. When we

transgressed, out slipped the belt. Having
chewed the nails of exile all through one
aching afternoon, we'd dread the gavel
footstep in the hall, deliberate as Sunday,
remote as a stranger at the door, knob
turning now, a judge stern as the Tower

of Babel but much more determined
to make himself understood. Nothing
between him and his message, no
beard, no smell, nothing on his breath but
the Word. That belt jumped with life
everlasting. What we recall is how he

looked right before the punishment, as God
must have looked, face blank as creation's
void, face teaching its love lesson the way
it's been done for centuries, he's sorry, he
doesn't want to hurt you. Ministrant, wreak
holy havoc upon the tiny ass of man, we who

defy the collection plate, saving the dime
for fortune's pocket. Somebody must strap
our badness, somebody must pry the dime

from our fist, somebody like the shadow
father you know is coming, huge and fair,
crew-cut, creaking the boards on Babel's stair.

The Aunts by Firelight

I.

Poor Jakob lolls sedated in his chair
between gray sisters, some crocheting shawls.
A photograph of them with braided hair
in which they stand like Matryoshka dolls,
all seventeen, a sober S in line
from eldest to youngest, is passed around.
Still in the world, they seem so far from mine!
They look down gently, as from holy ground.

The flames conserve their warmth like thrifty Dutch.
In harmony the aunts begin a hymn,
too wise to know that they've forgotten much
of the language lake in which I learned to swim—
a song as frail as wood smoke on the rise
that plumes the darkness, shadowing the eyes.

II

It plumes the darkness, shadowing the eyes,
this realization that our fathers' faith
hangs low through centuries that harmonize
with ours, a history vaporous as a wraith
appearing only when one's gravely ill.
The night is deepening. Now from wind-tossed
pines a bird, I think a whippoorwill,
repeats a mournful cry as if it's lost
some last ideal. Its moonlight quarterly
insists on tending branch, as I did once.
Resignation wears white shoes, an orderly
with papers one must sign. It's late. The aunts
are nodding off, a sleep that looks like prayer.
Poor Jakob lolls sedated in his chair.

Psalter Fool

dixit insipiens in corde suo non est deus

Calvo, calvino, deficient in
reason, incapable of negation and
affirmation, his is the ritualized
refusal of the Mercy Seat. Up he

springs from the Chair of Pestilence
to jest. Not for him, the long beards
of the holy; he shaves close to
the bone. And like a bone, he is

hungry. Ravenous, he hunches
greedily over a rock. See the
contro posto tearing of hair that is
not there: this frenetic hunger

cannot be fed. Dogs snap his heels.
Men point at their beards to mock
the club with which he denies justice.
Scorn against logos! *Populus*

lambens vel lingens, stones for
a licking people, earth-licking,
lingens terram, desiring earthen things.
Does the Fool smell the stink and shag

of the hirsute devil who holds the flesh
hook? And if the Fool puts down
his club and licks no more at his stone,
what does he wag but a finger stiff

with an inkling, an outrage
at bearded lies. Readers,
the Fool has never craved the stone.
He has found no bread he likes.

Tardy Elegy

for J.B., 1961-1992

Like guests who know when to leave,
the decades have gone from Lake Alice,
the hint of alligators, the dapper fringe

of cypress in white mist shirts.
What I didn't know then was
that I'd know you now. The lines

of your poems are a palm on which
a future appears fatidic, delectable:
tensile webbed profligacy, four

wives, the note found in a shoebox,
cocktails that could bay at the moon.
Words, my friend, are classmates tipsy

at a reunion. Therefore I seek you
in the absent margins, the space left
by that bastard Elgin. You, my familiar,

my purgatory where eyes kiss the ending
of a story implied but nonetheless left
loose, a labyrinth of baggy monsters.

On the shores of this island shagged
with palms, the tide pulls shallows
into sand, the very grain of sleep. Now

the sound of ice in a glass set down.
The bourbon is gone, but a distracted hand
picks up the glass and holds the ice

against the moonlight for who knows
what reason. They say in the south that
a man's drink melts his middle age.

Joe, you are the condensation under
the glass—odorless, colorless, the breath
that stirs the death in every life.

Point to the Pain with One Finger

Point to the pain with one finger,
says the surgeon some two months
after the hernia repair. Certainly

pain can be supportive; it calls
sociably for triple-shot martinis,
solicits Napoleonic posture, hand

on Personal Region, a refinement,
a sharpening of luck's little clippers.
For instance. You move to Chicago.

Day one, Starbucks. You spot
a woman you haven't seen in
seven years. This is the magic

of pain. Why Christine, you exclaim.
She smiles tentatively, married now,
willing to remember with a hint.

This is the woman who, when you
got the call that your dad was dying,
rustled up a thermos and a bag of

sandwiches in what seemed like
seconds. Just drive, she said, I'll
look after the cat. That cat died

in L.A. some years later and for
months you thought you saw him
on the windowsill, paws tucked

under his chest as if holding
a very small purse, taking up
just that corner of sky.

Nocturne

A man with guests in his home
looks out over his lawn and sees

weeds. The weeds yearn toward
lighted windows and see fireflies.

The fireflies concentrate on
making out the street but see

only each other. The hostess
inspects an elliptical dish of

goat-cheese tarts but sees
gray strands of highways

pulled together as in a crocheted
reticule, the opening as neat,

as clipped, as a lady saying oh!
The moon looks at the earth

and thinks she will knit it
a sweater, which the earth

will wear when the good moon
comes calling at Christmas.

The Rebus

Once in a spanking
game of racquetball
a meteoric wallop

punched a thigh.
Soon the thing
began to emit its

own heat, a terrible
sun. A molten
core declared itself,

cobalt-colored, ball-sized.
And a Saturn of
suggestion ringed it;

violet filaments frisked
the skin. Subsequently
leaf-greens filtered

a fireball of yellows.
The missile had been
small, but the bruise

grew lush as a canopy.
Amorphous distortions!
Thus, rebus-like,

the Rorschach's litotes
is scribbled over.
The palimpsest purples

with meaning, that note
to self under the pant
leg of the every day.

What to Save

Evening drops its starched hanky.
Silence helps itself to a thick slice
of banana bread. Now the distant

music of hounds, singing their
long good-bye. A raccoon
commences some nocturnal business,

and a red whimsy comes circling
the evening before, chickens
solemn as a cortege, a whippoorwill

between five and six announcing
that it is time to describe
the twilight, time to start

the evening you should save,
receipt of some forgotten need.
A Greek chorus of insects

waits in the wings with
a sound like a kiss on the cheek,
summer folding its things into

an overnighter with a cunning
zippered pocket for your valuable.
Polish it, wrap it in a Pima napkin—

you might need it later, who knows,
it might appreciate, it might contract
like a heart, it might shudder

like a weird anemone when
in the future you poke it. It might
teach you how to grieve.

The Host

Starling's head in confetti
of feathers, injured mouse

trailing innards like a
sentence not quite deleted,

junebug chirring on its back,
clumps of tiny wood-colored

bunny, blood plumes like
an unfinished Pollock, all

ailing and flapping failures
of the night: come in. Stain

my carpet. You are
welcome in this house.

And so under a civil couch
we rattle and spin, leaking

our fierce red messes.
Are you oozing, dissatisfied,

feverish, resentful, fractured
in feather or bone?

Then come in, come in,
make yourself at home.

Shadow's Pleasure

Obscene terrain
toward cement cell
or outhouse: f-words
advertised untraveled
worlds. I who had
just learned the best

(that is, the worst)
read the needy dark
for queen's cunt
of combinations:
fireflies befouled
the musty night with

graffiti ultra-nasty.
O fresh profanities!
Who would not
wonder why the
bright winged insults

had been fisted
at the sky? As on
a timeline with
marked scarcity
of event, we
slumbered bagged

inside our tent.
And all the tents
stood flanked
in line. We feared

the spiders; we
smelled the pine.

Variations on *der Schleif*

Aproned

Around the feverish pot
barn cats wheel, hungry.
Fire pinks that German skin;
eyebrows arch surprise
at braids lithe as buggy whips.

She smoothes her apron:
in spite of morning's starching,
it pleats a threadbare
ground with tiny cornflowers,
once alive and blue, now

faded to a plain unknowable
pattern, like freckles that
reconfigure according to the
tightness of her braids,
white feathers of eyebrows

in painful flight to join
a high and restive flock.
The bars stiffen to buff, pale
bricks broken with a sturdy knife.
(Years later she still calls

the spoon a Schleif.) Boiling
impatience, she stirs the Saturday
in endless revolution toward
that clean victory when bars of

sorrel and honey-smelling soap

snap clean. Her bath is last,
lit by kerosene. She dumps
a fresh kettle hung white
with restless steam: new soap.
Course cloth of a private dream.

In A Long-Sleeved Smock

Why should she recall
how to make soap?
At least she's careful
how she assumes
the rubber gloves.
She hopes Burn Day
allows it. Puzzled
by forgetfulness,
her forehead pinches
years. How much lye?
Where nowadays to get
the fat? On Sundays
in church, so stinging
clean she'd scratch....
But she finds her memory
has dissolved to a vague
murmur of bees
beating ripe apricots.
She can test the spots
where lye once
splashed her wrists,
the pucker of slug-white
medallions that toughened

silent stares. The burns
charm like a bracelet,
those discs engraved
for the brisk-hearted,
the squint-eyed,
the dowry-chested,
the never bride.

North Dakota Sestina

ending with a line from Psalm 19

Beyond the matchbook parsonage
in fields reduced to stubble,
the rows untangled, as if a comb
had pulled them taut. The sigh
of the wind, sad at harvest, came rolling
like an old-fashioned wagon wheel.

The Liebelts' combine wheeled
around the tiny parsonage,
the great machinery rolling
toward the stiff August stubble.
Hulling loganberries, the child sighed
as she watched the combine comb

the wheat. Mornings, Mother's comb
straightened, thus: the braided wheel
of hair loosened like a sigh.
Racing from the tidy parsonage
to the fields of wild stubble,
the girl, hot, began rolling

her long sleeves. She tripped, rolling
down the incline into a catacomb
of indifferent yellow stubble,
sharp as the spokes of a wheel.
Her mother, watching from the parsonage,
came running. And the child sighed,

as if in all the Dakotas one full sigh
could stop the stupid tears rolling
or the thought of the stiff parsonage
and the terrible pull of the comb.
The mother rolled her like a wheel,
to see the scratches from the stubble,

but the girl saw only the stubble
collapsing in the field. She heard the sigh
of the combine finishing summer, the wheel
of winter like a thunderous silo rolling.
In her hair she spread her hand like a comb
and pinched her eyes shut to the parsonage.

Hair scythed short as stubble, she'd cartwheel
the parsonage and land in the last field rolling,
with a sigh sweeter than honey or the honeycomb.

Man Answers God

Maschine Zur Vertilgung der Heuschrekken
—Johann Braun Archive, Kiev

They were working on a machine
that would inhale and annihilate
the locusts. Even on paper
it looked ominous: creaking wheels,

gears, penciled arrows to chart
wind movement, the funnel
with the sucking power, the black
rubber belt imported from

Germany. You would hear the tic
of contact, the blundering locusts
as they tried to pull back,
too late, hot air rushing oblivion,

extermination systematized in one
astonished pulse of the strawstick
insect heart, the wheat saved,
and August bearable again.

I'm told that it would have worked,
that they very nearly had it—
the wife as she hauled a tin bucket,
sweet peach Saft sloshing the sides,

must have wiped her damp hairline
as she approached the shed where they
were building the terrible engine.
The zinging collision of wings on skin

once would have made her shriek
with the proper panic of her sex, but
now she mechanically slaps and stuns.
She scoops them as they splashland

in the bucket, and flicks them wetly
to the ground. She has a case
of the heatshimmers: the field
is undulating under the iridescent

whir of locusts. All, all, feasting
on the future that should be hers.
It is their land; they work the wheat.
It is a plague, she thinks, a judgment

on riotous living, and it is well
that man answers God with a machine
that will rid the world of locusts
forever, steel cylinders chuffing.

Heavy Yellow Heads

Saint Sophia's Byzantine mosaics show
the heads of saints balancing gold Frisbees,
or cumbrous yellow pleated into rays
so heavy that heads bend like slender stems
of sunflowers. Broad yellow still strokes heads
cocked sunward, nodding wisely in the breeze,
as if these, generations later, can
remember hurried graves and tangled roots,
the family that heard of troops in Schönsee,
and knew their village would be next. Parents

whisper the sound of leafy stalks, rustling,
darkness curling corners, twilight pushing
like a bully, pictures knotted into
hankies, zwieback counted and wrapped, rubles
pocket-pinned, floorboards pried to hide the last
watermelon syrup since the sugar
ran out. Father explains that they will go
to the sunflower fields, sleep on the ground—
like Cossacks? the boy wants to know, and his
father affirms, Yes, like Cossacks. They will

be quiet as cats, and unlike Cossacks
they will pray. The oldest nods, suspecting,
turns his brother's little lion torso
and buttons his play-soiled blouse and smiles hard.
In the long damp Rudy sleeps fitfully,
starting awake to surprise a round moon
on the rise like a bun. His father, still
awake, puts a finger to lips that say,
Amen. Sleep now because when the light comes

pink and cautious over the sunflowers

the bayonets will find me. Your brother
will die neatly of the cholera, your
mother will survive the rapes to ghost your
middle-age, lips moving silently as
in rhythmic rocking on your patio
she prays mercy, mercy, mercy. But you,
my son, alight on a wagonbed of
corpses, brush away the sweet-rot odor
like a moth, hop down smartly at the train.
I predict that the stars will favor you,

that you will at sixty-three return on
a Mennonite Heritage Tour. And when
our muddy country roads confound your bus,
try bribing peasants on their motorbikes
to bump you back to Alexanderfeld.
Don't forget this map. Find your childhood home.
Give to the babushka (your childhood friend)
some kopeks to see the casual hens,
the mouldering walls, the very mattress where
you were born, the rat on its way, the hole

in the floor where your wife pants, There it is,
after all these years, the jar still rosy
with sluggish watermelon syrup. Bend
and inhale—ah, it is fragrant July,
it is your final cup of tea sweetened
with the heart of summer melons, it is
pink uncomplicated breath of babies

asleep in a field of fear beneath a
broken zwieback moon, and one half hugging
the sky, the other already eaten,

the urgent hunger for more, the crumbs that
fall to earth, to the fields of sunflowers.
In unison melancholy, these bow
their heavy yellow heads to the broken
bread of remembrance. The stars are crumbs
falling whitely into mouths that open
galaxies, and sunflowers stoop under
onus of what shoulders can bear: they have
a long way to Byzantium, pale roots
trailing, heads gold-tipped and insatiable.

Sum of All Parts

Bad Breath

Foul secret that blasts
the palm, it confesses age,
the peculiar workings of
the gums. With what
savoir-faire it alludes

to tongue and tonsil!
Somewhere in the darkness
hangs the uvula, velvet
scrotal orchid in its
hothouse of suggestion.

Bad breath plumps
your cushion, whisks away
an invisible crumb. Trust it
like an instinct. It cannot
fail you. It is like a jovial

rich gentleman whose
company you will enjoy.
See, it is opening
a program in the red plush
theater of your mouth.

A bowtie scuds its chins.
Here is the sound of
fluttering strings and
low inquisitive horns.
Hush, the thing begins.

Varicose Vein

The femoral vein's refulgent
urgency hurtles crotchward
to the heavenly symphasis pubis.
Like a blue behemoth it dithers

yon and hence at the knee,
beyond sense, as if it can't make
up its mind, or has no mind at all.
It seemed to sprout overnight,

purpling the leg, a roiling storm.
The trunk is huge and fleshy,
a Lombard in travail. *Cielo,
aiutame!* Lord, it's big! At least

wait until nightfall. Sleep and
study; take your knowledge and
your knife. There may appear
a traveler who without preamble

will challenge you to a match.
Checkmate him with your queen:
victory demands his cunning little
valuable. As you climb, expect

to ossify like the vein itself,
ancient but spry, your hair
the color of driftwood, your skin
burled hard as a root. Like blue

blood slugged to the heart
by threadlike valves that nudge it
infinitesimally upward, you can't
come back. Let me therefore kiss

your cheek farewell. Draw near
and let me queer your face once
more, O hirsute daughter. Let me pet
your curly sideburns and your beard.

Frizzy Hair

Guard the gorgon of restlessness
that grows beyond death like
Methuselah. Flyaways shed

the indeterminate color of ash.
Like the magician, I admit to charm.
In my hand I hold only a hissing

flatiron. What sleight-of-hand that
lightens the deathhead's bristling
nap! Right before your eyes the ends

are sealed. Taut as a cocoon, sweeter
also than honey, straightened hair
is like the apotropaic masks of ancient

Greece, those worn on the stage of
Sophocles. In assuming their disguise,
the players alluded to the semitragedy

of saltatory change. The actors must
have been surprised to learn that once
they donned a mask, they could never

take it off. Such masks graft muscle
memory. The occipital extrusion
sockets a disguise that rides the naked

face like the tiny but relentless
spasm of an amputated limb. Pale as
Rapunzel, my hair licks the fingers

deliciously. It is a silk purse bursting
with doubloons. See with what witchery
its golden snood will hold your stone

when you, looking over your shoulder
but finding yourself alone, test a handful,
exactly as the oracle said you would.

Winter Skin

In the bathroom at work
you suddenly notice a fine
white alkali on your thighs,
a winter desert, the tundra

chap in which you could
write a prophesy. Your
legs are spidershanks,
the dermis so dry you

could spin it like flax
into gold. Here in your
little locked chamber
time sifts swiftly through

its glass. You had better
hurry—Aigruchonne is coming.
Spin furiously, O miller's
daughter. Under your skin

the bones bleach thin as
whiskers, bones that will
lodge in a valley of bones,
bones that will scour your

centuries. Pubis, femur,
patella, tibia—peaceably
dry, they lie in the sand
of your limbs. Along comes

Ezekiel. Let him cry to
the wind, Where, O Lord,
is the knucklebone, where
the sinew, where the skin?

Plantar's Wart

Hard as a hoof, ball of the foot,
slough that you shave blood-thin
before the freeze. If not dimethyl
ether, laser. If not laser,

jawbone. Limp and hobble,
weird sister, sorceress of Sorek,
shaggy harlot who lopes back
night after night. *De profundis*

the fungus returns, a spot of taint
that's bugshell tough. It's the pea
some curious king has slipped
beneath your mattress stack.

Princess, pebble your royal hissyfit.
Witchfooted, it comes burning
like Ataragis to Ascalon. Dea Syria,
this leprosy shoots, tiny seed of

poison that promulgates its woody
surge. I'll tell you why you can't get
rid of it. Snug core of spoiled self,
it pesters the sole. Contagion divides

and multiplies like lice. Vice, device—
Delilah turns to you at 3:00 a.m.,
saying, Let me take a little off the sides.
The plantar flaws the foundation,

fractured now by a riddle subtle as
a hairline crack: out of the eater, meat,
and out of the strong, sweet. Incantatory
cootie, it's small as a nit, brown as

a louse. Don't pry it out, or you'll
be forced to heave the temple down,
shorn and warted, judge whose last
big thrust brings down the house.

Recurring Rash

Like the semaphore swords
of cherubim guarding
paradise, the spots
prognosticate. Note the

charmed honeysuckle
that thorns the perimeter.
The rash advances and retreats
like Lilith, glad to be gone but

refusing to believe that she's
locked out. In the garden's
Rorschach you detect the shape
of a maiden who is half-sick

of shadows—no, a pig, and see,
she's eating her young. Look
without reading, stare to the end.
(Guido says the ending could be

big.) But even as a flickering
tongue of comprehension cusps,
the rash vanishes into your hat,
into your hair, into the leaves

of the knowledge tree, where
each purled branch could be
a snake. Without fear of
infamy I speak, since the gods,

in sympathy with the ignorance
that keeps you scratching
your head, have thoughtfully
turned you into a lawn

onto whose tended green
every doggone spring
a patch of crab comes
grinning back like Banquo.

Odorous Crotch

Like the lodestone of regret,
the odorous crotch smells
solitude. The toilet seats

civilization's edge. Now
the odor like a telegram
from Rangoon, some damp

and distant interior: O my
daughter, how can I ever
ask you to forgive? Eerie,

delicate, now you smell it.
You can almost taste the acrid
tickle that waters the mouth

like a Popsicle. Bow your
head. Sniff it. It is everything
from which truth depends,

reminding us as we sigh
to be clean that some things
cannot be cleansed, things

so hot they're cold, the line
between extremes absurd as
Limburger furred with mold.

Pinched Nerve

Pain in the neck, balled on the back
like a hobo's sack swinging from the stick
of your spine. Down to hell and back, you

ride the moonlit rails, the whistle tooting its
lonely ache. At dawn the door slides open
in a landscape familiar as a nightmare that,

friendly-like, suggests you watch your back.
Sure enough, the maenads are on the prowl
with their weird little hatchets, sharp enough

to hack you into nine even pieces. Howl
like a jackal, moan like an owl! Each piece
contains its share of muscle, bone, and nerve.

The senior maenad takes the head, pinched
nerve dangling from the neck. She sets out
for Tucson, kissing her sisters goodbye,

invoking a Dionysian blessing, achieving
ecstasy in a whirling type of dance—a series
of formalities to which you, being dead,

remain indifferent. When she arrives, half
of Tucson is on fire, danger dipping down
the mountain. The maenad gets as close

as she can stand, tongues of flame snapping
sassy as a garter belt, the heat outrageous,
redhot as porn. With all her might she heaves

your head and nerve into the conflagration
and says to no one in particular, Burn, baby,
burn. That should do it. Next time you'll learn.

Itchy Ear

A scabrous itchy ear,
the same ear, simplifies
desire. Pull at it, scratch

it till it bleeds, pretend
it is not odd to have
this itchy ear. Consult

no doctor, tug at it when
alone. Friend, facts
frame your face like ears.

Desire will not cease
to itch. Helplessly fixed
between sight and speech,

portal to mystery, the ears
recall Blake's *Gates*
of Hell. Itch loopdeloops

in serpentine folds like
a miniature melusina,
needy siren who shakes

her tail at those who
think they can cut it off.
Can't cure it, can't say

what it has heard.
Pink flap crawling with
itch like flies on curd.

Epic Bruise

Bruises burst lickety-split,
slick as a swirling flume
contused, swearing up

a blue streak down the leg.
Here is the blue cap
of an archipelago adrift

to some unknown Atlantis
on the calf. This one bleats
like a golden ewe about to be

clipped—oh, angry!—ruffling
like an outraged bird that has
been flipped so turgidly

the digit shakes. No bruise
is what it seems, a simple
aftermath. What we need

is an interpreter of dreams
and signs, a Daniel whose eye
decodes the wrath. Though

sudden, it can plan. Much
struck, it will strike. Bring it on,
it mutters under its breath

like Atreus watching in cartoon
glee as his brother sucks
the pith from a bone. Hehheh,

he's gone and done it, he's
eaten his own! Now give
that guy a hand, a hand and

a foot to be exact. Don't
fuck with me. Once out,
the choler can't come back.

Engorged Breast

Like the whisker of
an ancient fish, its
nipple frisks the air.

The spectacular breast
is the size of a head,
a head with a mind

and a plan that asserts
contemplation and time,
time spent becalmed

on a bed where even
at night one wears a bra
tough as a rubber raft.

Cold-blooded, it lolls
on the chest. Queasy, it
sickens the sheets.

Hold on—it is making
a move. From out of
the heaving seas

it rises and swallows me
whole. Inside it is red,
it is dark, and it smells

of a drip. It may even
detect my regret, all
those things that I said

of the Lord. My friend,
meet me in Tarsus if
you ever get this card.

Frown Line

A tectonic fault splits the forehead.
The Big One comes to the California
of my head; my face drops off

into the sea. What remains is a new
Gold Coast, one glorious undisputed
eye training its beam like a lighthouse

from a cliff. It shines on all stormy
seas. Here comes Margaret Fuller
with a babe and a guy she swears

she married. The Plan B captain,
the one who didn't die of smallpox,
sounds the alarm. Margaret neatly zips

her *Complete History of The Italian
Revolution* into a waterproof baggie.
Then Ossoli hands her Angelo while

he yanks off her bombazine skirt and
crinoline, cuts her stays with a penknife.
(He may be a lousy sculptor, but he

knows what to do in a storm.) Now
she clings to him in her thin chemise.
Holding her face between his hands,

he kisses her once on the mouth before
handing her into the lifeboat. *Ti amo,*

he calls encouragingly. *Posso ancora*

vederti! Now by the power of my
needle eye, I thread the fog, give
Margaret hope. No one has to die.

Untimely Cramp

Shuddering interloper, it spooks
the horses of the spine. Phaeton
snaps his whip; hubris cracks;
doomsday hisses and spits. It's

coming. Apollo, predictable,
hurls thunderbolts. Hot, then
creepycold—don't take it
personally. The question,

Clymene: Are you prepared?
Presentiment comes galloping
from the corners of your chill.
Something's in there bucking

like an urgent ouija board. Let's
hold hands. Like a dear departed
wife in the spirit world, it floats up
to lay one light and misty is it arm?

atop your knees. Uh-oh, the table
is rising and knocking. Spirit,
loose and dying Zeitgeist,
intercede for us. Let these

tremors cease. I think I see
the ghost in the machine—she's
huge, she's blonde. White lips
freak warning from beyond.

Enlarged Pore

One day I was in the Spirit and I heard
behind me a thundering voice
like a trumpet, a child's toy,
saying, Write on a scroll with this sword

what you see, and send it to seven friends,
who will each send it to seven more,
and so on. I saw in the magnified lens
the one spot my arm forbore

to reach, and it sat like white itch
on the vanishing point between
the double-edged twitch
of my shoulders: a speck like a queen

on the throne of the back, spot whose
guile twisted back to the portal,
dolorous door to the house of blues
that virgins penetrate, immortal.

Inside its gates the streets were paved
with gracious gold behavior.
Then I suddenly felt saved,
and I saw a white-robed savior

winking with a thousand convivial eyes,
saying, Come, spotted and carnelian ladies,
the carousel revolves! Reach for the prize,
the massy keys I hold to Hades.

Broken Talus

Like an igneous
wiggling in ancient
catacombs of molten

rock, the talus,
broken so long ago,
asserts a liquid pain.

Little halfwit of bone,
it didn't know to knit
itself to itself.

The foot is long
and locked, a
Russian reliquary

guarded in venerable
monasteries beneath
Odessa. In holy

synecdoche it cradles
the shard of a saint
martyred six hundred

years ago on the steps
of Saint Sophia's.
The bone, ready to

resurrect, says, We are
not broken to heal,
else we would heal.

No: we are broken
to exhume the very
aches we die to feel.